This Recipe Book Belongs To:

A Collection of My Favorite Recipes

Table of Contents

Page	Recipe Name

Table of Contents

Page	Recipe Name

Table of Contents

Page	Recipe Name

Recipe:

Serves: Prep Time: Cook Time: Cook Temp:

Ingredients:

Directions:

Notes:

Recipe: ______________________________

Serves: ________ Prep Time: ________ Cook Time: ________ Cook Temp: ________

Ingredients:

Directions:

Notes:

Recipe:

Serves: Prep Time: Cook Time: Cook Temp:

Ingredients:

Directions:

Notes:

4

Recipe: ______________________________

Serves: ________ Prep Time: ________ Cook Time: ________ Cook Temp: ________

Ingredients:

Directions:

Notes:

Recipe: ______

Serves: ______ Prep Time: ______ Cook Time: ______ Cook Temp: ______

Ingredients:

Directions:

Notes:

Recipe:

Serves: Prep Time: Cook Time: Cook Temp:

Ingredients:

Directions:

Notes:

Recipe:

Serves: Prep Time: Cook Time: Cook Temp:

Ingredients:

Directions:

Notes:

Recipe: ____________________

Serves: ________ Prep Time: ________ Cook Time: ________ Cook Temp: ________

Ingredients:

Directions:

Notes:

Recipe: ______________________________

Serves: ________ Prep Time: ________ Cook Time: ________ Cook Temp: ________

Ingredients:

Directions:

Notes:

Recipe: ______________________________

Serves: ________ Prep Time: ________ Cook Time: ________ Cook Temp: ________

Ingredients:

Directions:

Notes:

Recipe: ______

Serves: ______ Prep Time: ______ Cook Time: ______ Cook Temp: ______

Ingredients:

Directions:

Notes:

Recipe: ______________________________

Serves: ________ Prep Time: ________ Cook Time: ________ Cook Temp: ________

Ingredients:

Directions:

Notes:

Recipe: ______

Serves: ______ Prep Time: ______ Cook Time: ______ Cook Temp: ______

Ingredients:

Directions:

Notes:

Recipe: ____________________

Serves: ________ Prep Time: ________ Cook Time: ________ Cook Temp: ________

Ingredients:

Directions:

Notes:

Recipe:

Serves: Prep Time: Cook Time: Cook Temp:

Ingredients:

Directions:

Notes:

Recipe: ______

Serves: ______ Prep Time: ______ Cook Time: ______ Cook Temp: ______

Ingredients:

Directions:

Notes:

Recipe: ____________________

Serves: ________ Prep Time: ________ Cook Time: ________ Cook Temp: ________

Ingredients:

Directions:

Notes:

Recipe: ______________________________

Serves: ________ Prep Time: ________ Cook Time: ________ Cook Temp: ________

Ingredients:

Directions:

Notes:

Recipe:

Serves: Prep Time: Cook Time: Cook Temp:

Ingredients:

Directions:

Notes:

Recipe: ______

Serves: ______ Prep Time: ______ Cook Time: ______ Cook Temp: ______

Ingredients:

Directions:

Notes:

Recipe: ____________________

Serves: ________ Prep Time: ________ Cook Time: ________ Cook Temp: ________

Ingredients:

Directions:

Notes:

Recipe:

Serves: Prep Time: Cook Time: Cook Temp:

Ingredients:

Directions:

Notes:

Recipe: ______________________________

Serves: ________ Prep Time: ________ Cook Time: ________ Cook Temp: ________

Ingredients:

Directions:

Notes:

Recipe: ______

Serves: ______ Prep Time: ______ Cook Time: ______ Cook Temp: ______

Ingredients:

Directions:

Notes:

Recipe:

Serves: Prep Time: Cook Time: Cook Temp:

Ingredients:

Directions:

Notes:

Recipe: ____________________

Serves: ________ Prep Time: ________ Cook Time: ________ Cook Temp: ________

Ingredients:

Directions:

Notes:

Recipe:

Serves: Prep Time: Cook Time: Cook Temp:

Ingredients:

Directions:

Notes:

Recipe: ______________________________

Serves: ________ Prep Time: ________ Cook Time: ________ Cook Temp: ________

Ingredients:

Directions:

Notes:

Recipe: ______________________________

Serves: ________ Prep Time: ________ Cook Time: ________ Cook Temp: ________

Ingredients:

Directions:

Notes:

Recipe:

Serves: Prep Time: Cook Time: Cook Temp:

Ingredients:

Directions:

Notes:

Recipe: ______________________________

Serves: ________ Prep Time: ________ Cook Time: ________ Cook Temp: ________

Ingredients:

Directions:

Notes:

Recipe: ______________________________

Serves: ________ Prep Time: ________ Cook Time: ________ Cook Temp: ________

Ingredients:

Directions:

Notes:

Recipe: ______________________________

Serves: ________ Prep Time: ________ Cook Time: ________ Cook Temp: ________

Ingredients:

Directions:

Notes:

Recipe: ____________________

Serves: ________ Prep Time: ________ Cook Time: ________ Cook Temp: ________

Ingredients:

Directions:

Notes:

Recipe: ______________________________

Serves: ________ Prep Time: ________ Cook Time: ________ Cook Temp: ________

Ingredients:

Directions:

Notes:

Recipe:

Serves: ________ Prep Time: ________ Cook Time: ________ Cook Temp: ________

Ingredients:

Directions:

Notes:

Recipe: ____________________

Serves: ________ Prep Time: ________ Cook Time: ________ Cook Temp: ________

Ingredients:

Directions:

Notes:

Recipe: ____________________

Serves: ______ Prep Time: ______ Cook Time: ______ Cook Temp: ______

Ingredients:

Directions:

Notes:

Recipe:

Serves: Prep Time: Cook Time: Cook Temp:

Ingredients:

Directions:

Notes:

Recipe: ______________________________

Serves: ________ Prep Time: ________ Cook Time: ________ Cook Temp: ________

Ingredients:

Directions:

Notes:

Recipe: ______

Serves: ______ Prep Time: ______ Cook Time: ______ Cook Temp: ______

Ingredients:

Directions:

Notes:

Recipe: ____________________

Serves: ______ Prep Time: ______ Cook Time: ______ Cook Temp: ______

Ingredients:

Directions:

Notes:

Recipe:

Serves: Prep Time: Cook Time: Cook Temp:

Ingredients:

Directions:

Notes:

Recipe: ______

Serves: ______ Prep Time: ______ Cook Time: ______ Cook Temp: ______

Ingredients:

Directions:

Notes:

Recipe:

Serves: Prep Time: Cook Time: Cook Temp:

Ingredients:

Directions:

Notes:

Recipe: ____________________

Serves: ________ Prep Time: ________ Cook Time: ________ Cook Temp: ________

Ingredients:

Directions:

Notes:

Recipe: ____________________

Serves: ________ Prep Time: ________ Cook Time: ________ Cook Temp: ________

Ingredients:

Directions:

Notes:

Recipe: ____

Serves: ________ Prep Time: ________ Cook Time: ________ Cook Temp: ________

Ingredients:

Directions:

Notes:

Recipe:

Serves: Prep Time: Cook Time: Cook Temp:

Ingredients:

Directions:

Notes:

Recipe:

Serves: Prep Time: Cook Time: Cook Temp:

Ingredients:

Directions:

Notes:

Recipe: ______

Serves: ______ Prep Time: ______ Cook Time: ______ Cook Temp: ______

Ingredients:

Directions:

Notes:

Recipe:

Serves: Prep Time: Cook Time: Cook Temp:

Ingredients:

Directions:

Notes:

Recipe: ______

Serves: ______ Prep Time: ______ Cook Time: ______ Cook Temp: ______

Ingredients:

Directions:

Notes:

Recipe: ______________________________

Serves: ________ Prep Time: ________ Cook Time: ________ Cook Temp: ________

Ingredients:

Directions:

Notes:

Recipe: ____________________

Serves: ________ Prep Time: ________ Cook Time: ________ Cook Temp: ________

Ingredients:

Directions:

Notes:

Recipe: ____________________

Serves: ________ Prep Time: ________ Cook Time: ________ Cook Temp: ________

Ingredients:

Directions:

Notes:

Recipe: ______________________________

Serves: ________ Prep Time: ________ Cook Time: ________ Cook Temp: ________

Ingredients:

Directions:

Notes:

Recipe:

Serves: Prep Time: Cook Time: Cook Temp:

Ingredients:

Directions:

Notes:

Recipe:

Serves: Prep Time: Cook Time: Cook Temp:

Ingredients:

Directions:

Notes:

Recipe: ______________________________

Serves: ________ Prep Time: ________ Cook Time: ________ Cook Temp: ________

Ingredients:

Directions:

Notes:

Recipe: ______________________

Serves: ________ Prep Time: ________ Cook Time: ________ Cook Temp: ________

Ingredients:

Directions:

Notes:

Recipe: ____________________

Serves: ________ Prep Time: ________ Cook Time: ________ Cook Temp: ________

Ingredients:

Directions:

Notes:

Recipe: ______________________________

Serves: ________ Prep Time: ________ Cook Time: ________ Cook Temp: ________

Ingredients:

Directions:

Notes:

Recipe: ______________________________

Serves: ________ Prep Time: ________ Cook Time: ________ Cook Temp: ________

Ingredients:

Directions:

Notes:

Recipe: ______________________________

Serves: ________ Prep Time: ________ Cook Time: ________ Cook Temp: ________

Ingredients:

Directions:

Notes:

Recipe: ______________________

Serves: ________ Prep Time: ________ Cook Time: ________ Cook Temp: ________

Ingredients:

Directions:

Notes:

Recipe: ______

Serves: ______ Prep Time: ______ Cook Time: ______ Cook Temp: ______

Ingredients:

Directions:

Notes:

Recipe: ______________________________

Serves: ________ Prep Time: ________ Cook Time: ________ Cook Temp: ________

Ingredients:

Directions:

Notes:

Recipe: ____________________

Serves: ________ Prep Time: ________ Cook Time: ________ Cook Temp: ________

Ingredients:

Directions:

Notes:

Recipe: ______________________________

Serves: ________ Prep Time: ________ Cook Time: ________ Cook Temp: ________

Ingredients:

Directions:

Notes:

Recipe: ____________________

Serves: ________ Prep Time: ________ Cook Time: ________ Cook Temp: ________

Ingredients:

Directions:

Notes:

Recipe: ______________________________

Serves: ________ Prep Time: ________ Cook Time: ________ Cook Temp: ________

Ingredients:

Directions:

Notes:

Recipe: ______

Serves: ______ Prep Time: ______ Cook Time: ______ Cook Temp: ______

Ingredients:

Directions:

Notes:

Recipe: ______________________________

Serves: ________ Prep Time: ________ Cook Time: ________ Cook Temp: ________

Ingredients:

Directions:

Notes:

Recipe: ______________________

Serves: ________ Prep Time: ________ Cook Time: ________ Cook Temp: ________

Ingredients:

Directions:

Notes:

Recipe: ______________________________

Serves: ________ Prep Time: ________ Cook Time: ________ Cook Temp: ________

Ingredients:

Directions:

Notes:

Recipe: ____________________

Serves: ________ Prep Time: ________ Cook Time: ________ Cook Temp: ________

Ingredients:

Directions:

Notes:

Recipe:

Serves: Prep Time: Cook Time: Cook Temp:

Ingredients:

Directions:

Notes:

Recipe: ____________________

Serves: ______ Prep Time: ______ Cook Time: ______ Cook Temp: ______

Ingredients:

Directions:

Notes:

Recipe: ______________________________

Serves: ________ Prep Time: ________ Cook Time: ________ Cook Temp: ________

Ingredients:

Directions:

Notes:

Recipe: ______________________________

Serves: ________ Prep Time: ________ Cook Time: ________ Cook Temp: ________

Ingredients:

Directions:

Notes:

Recipe: ______________________________

Serves: ________ Prep Time: ________ Cook Time: ________ Cook Temp: ________

Ingredients:

Directions:

Notes:

Recipe: ______

Serves: ______ Prep Time: ______ Cook Time: ______ Cook Temp: ______

Ingredients:

Directions:

Notes:

Recipe: ______

Serves: ______ Prep Time: ______ Cook Time: ______ Cook Temp: ______

Ingredients:

Directions:

Notes:

Recipe: ______________________________

Serves: ________ Prep Time: ________ Cook Time: ________ Cook Temp: ________

Ingredients:

Directions:

Notes:

Recipe: ______________________________

Serves: ________ Prep Time: ________ Cook Time: ________ Cook Temp: ________

Ingredients:

Directions:

Notes:

Recipe: ______________________

Serves: ______ Prep Time: ______ Cook Time: ______ Cook Temp: ______

Ingredients:

Directions:

Notes:

Recipe: ____________________

Serves: ________ Prep Time: ________ Cook Time: ________ Cook Temp: ________

Ingredients:

Directions:

Notes:

Recipe: ____________________

Serves: ______ Prep Time: ______ Cook Time: ______ Cook Temp: ______

Ingredients:

Directions:

Notes:

Recipe: ______________________________

Serves: ________ Prep Time: ________ Cook Time: ________ Cook Temp: ________

Ingredients:

Directions:

Notes:

Recipe: ____________________

Serves: ________ Prep Time: ________ Cook Time: ________ Cook Temp: ________

Ingredients:

Directions:

Notes:

Recipe: ______________________________

Serves: ________ Prep Time: ________ Cook Time: ________ Cook Temp: ________

Ingredients:

Directions:

Notes:

Recipe: ____________________

Serves: ________ Prep Time: ________ Cook Time: ________ Cook Temp: ________

Ingredients:

Directions:

Notes:

Recipe: ______________________________

Serves: ________ Prep Time: ________ Cook Time: ________ Cook Temp: ________

Ingredients:

Directions:

Notes:

Recipe: ____________________

Serves: ______ Prep Time: ______ Cook Time: ______ Cook Temp: ______

Ingredients:

Directions:

Notes:

Made in the USA
Las Vegas, NV
01 June 2022

49598586R00057